AF291710

Usborne

All you need to know about Our World by age 7

Alice James

Illustrated by Stefano Tognetti

Designed by Alice Reese

Edited by Katie Daynes
Series editor: Rosie Dickins
Series designer: Zoe Wray

Geography expert: Penny Coltman

Contents

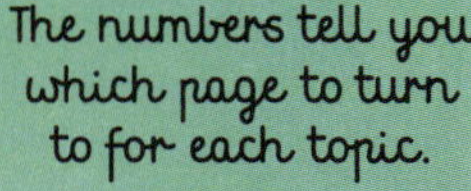

For links to websites where you can explore the world, watch wild animals and find out how to help our planet with videos, virtual tours, quizzes and games, go to usborne.com/Quicklinks and type in the title of this book. Children should be supervised online.

I'm Dragonfly! I'm about to fly all over the world. Turn the pages to follow my adventures...

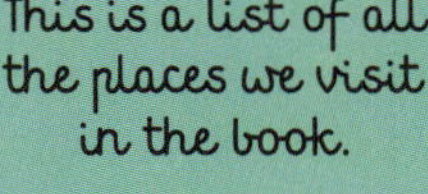

This is a list of all the places we visit in the book.

If you can't find what you're looking for in the contents list, try searching the index on page 80.

Welcome to our world

This round ball is our home. It's pretty special.
It's called Planet Earth.

You share it with over 8 billion other people.

You also share it with all sorts of different types of animals and plants...

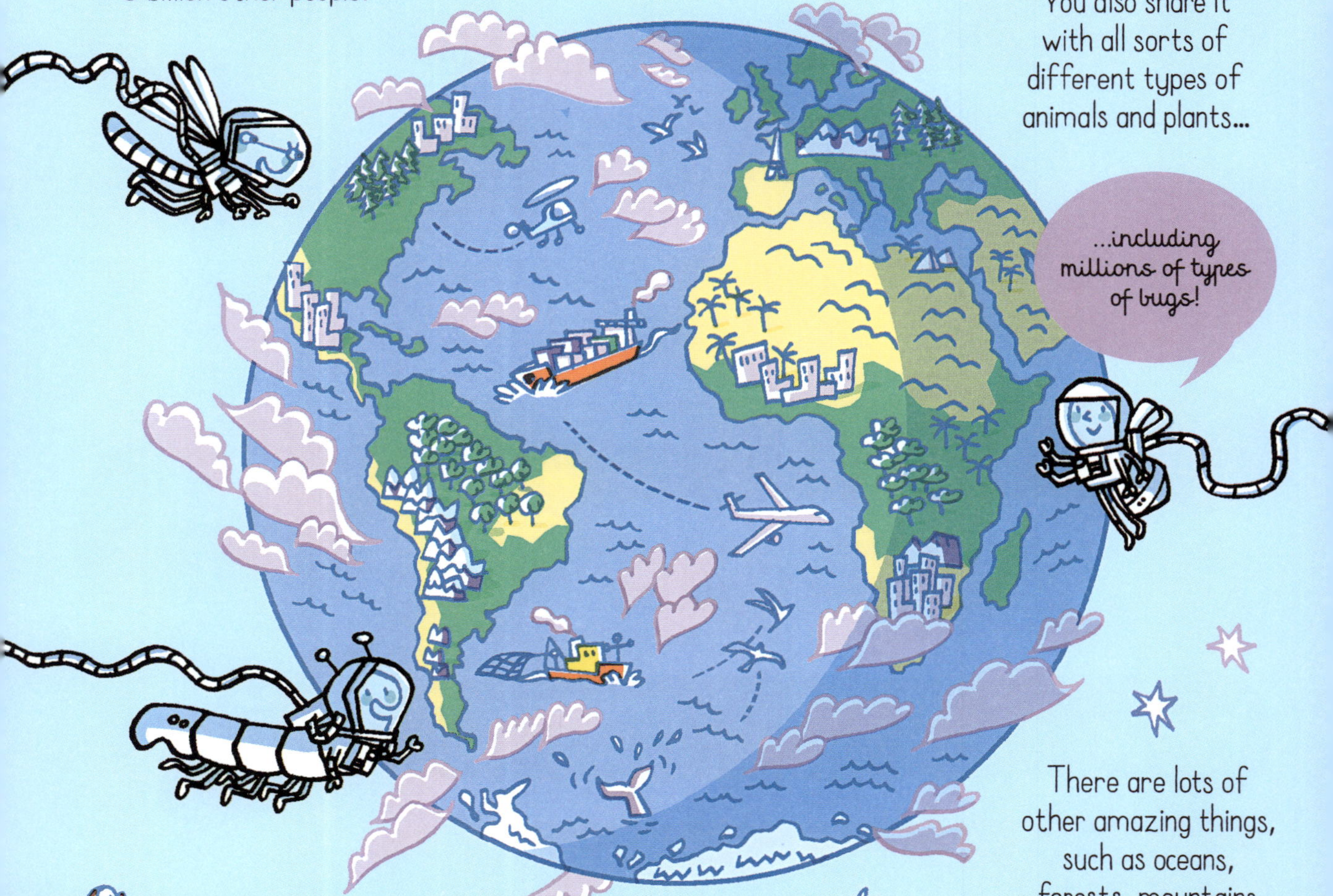

There are lots of other amazing things, such as oceans, forests, mountains and the weather.

Earth is the ONLY planet we know of that has things living on it – so we need to look after it.

For thousands of years, we have been asking questions about our world.

Over time, people have discovered more and more about the world.
Here are some of the ways they show other people what they know.

MAPS

MAPS are like flattened-out globes.
Being flat makes them easier to read and carry around.

6

DATA

Information about our world is called DATA. It's collected through fieldwork, which means going out and asking questions to find answers. Here are some ways of doing that.

Studying the world is called GEOGRAPHY.
Geography tells us about...

Planet Earth

Our world is one of many planets in space.
From space, it looks a little like this...

It doesn't feel like it, but the Earth is constantly moving.

It moves in a big circle called an ORBIT around the Sun.

One orbit takes a whole YEAR.

There are seven other planets that share our Sun.

SUN

EARTH

MOON

The Moon goes around the Earth.

The Earth is just far enough away from the Sun that it's not too hot and not too cold. It's just right for life.

As well as going around the Sun, the Earth also SPINS around.

It's DAY on the part of the Earth facing the Sun...

...and NIGHT on the part of the Earth facing away.

Mercury

Venus

Earth

Mars

Jupiter

Saturn

Uranus

Neptune

Pluto is so tiny it's called a DWARF planet.

Pluto

9

Land and sea

The world's LAND is split up into seven main areas, called CONTINENTS.
The water is split up into five huge OCEANS.

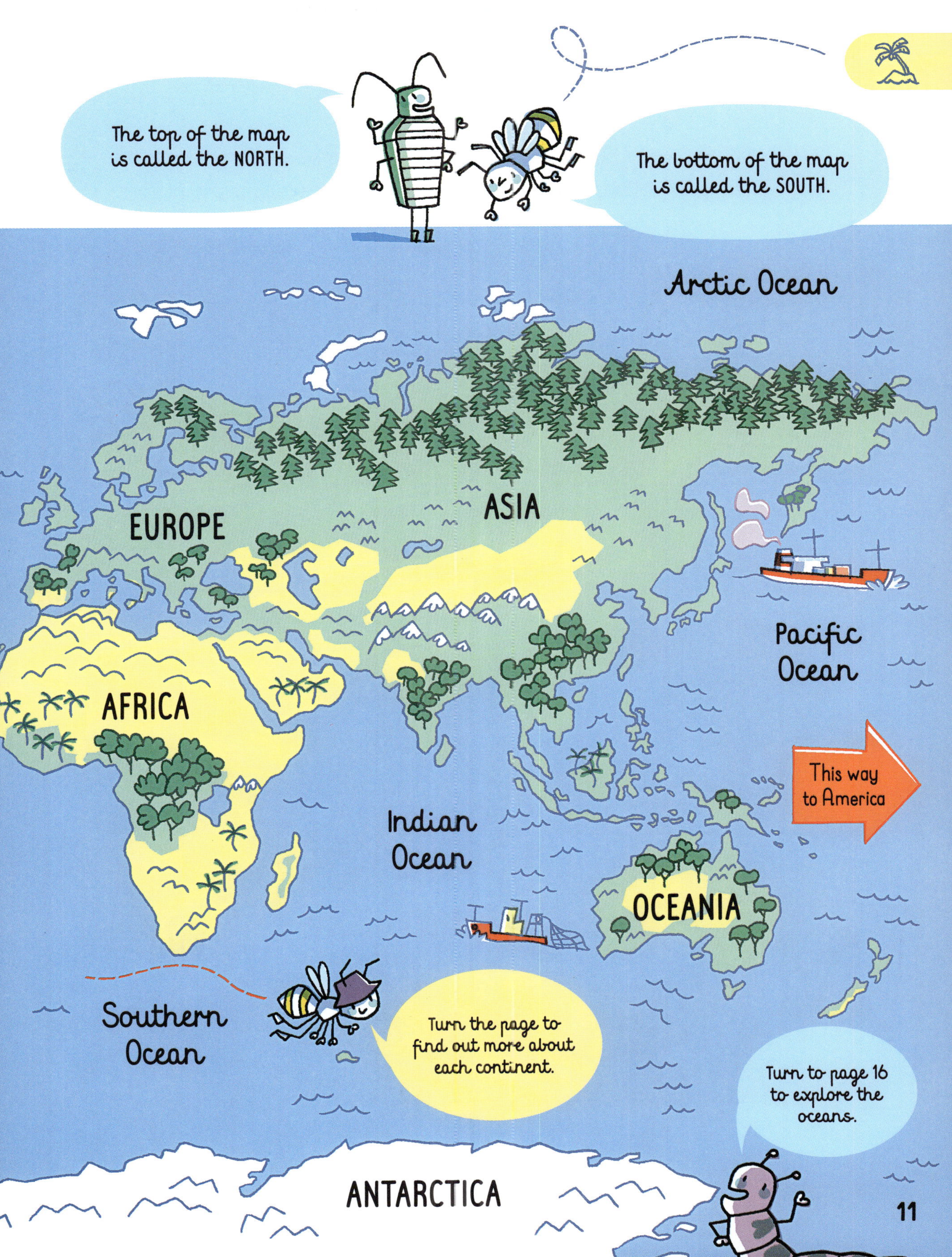

The top of the map is called the NORTH.
The bottom of the map is called the SOUTH.
Arctic Ocean
ASIA
EUROPE
Pacific Ocean
AFRICA
This way to America
Indian Ocean
OCEANIA
Turn the page to find out more about each continent.
Southern Ocean
Turn to page 16 to explore the oceans.
ANTARCTICA
11

Continents

The continents are HUGE. Each of them has been changed by the people who live there, and they all have their own amazing wildlife and nature.

ASIA

Asia is the BIGGEST continent. It has busy cities and more people than any other continent.

AFRICA

Africa's animals live in hot deserts and grasslands, muddy riverbanks and steamy jungles.

Africa was home to the first ever people.

It contains some amazing ancient monuments.

EUROPE

Europe has all sorts of cities, old and new, and lots of famous landmarks.

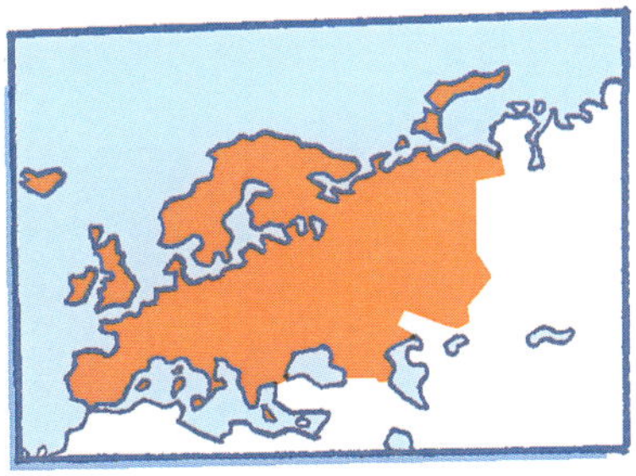

For many weeks, the far north is dark and frozen.

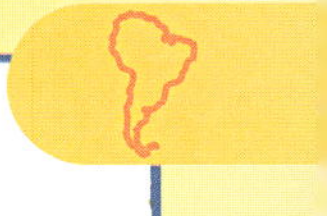

Parthenon Temple, Greece

NORTH AMERICA

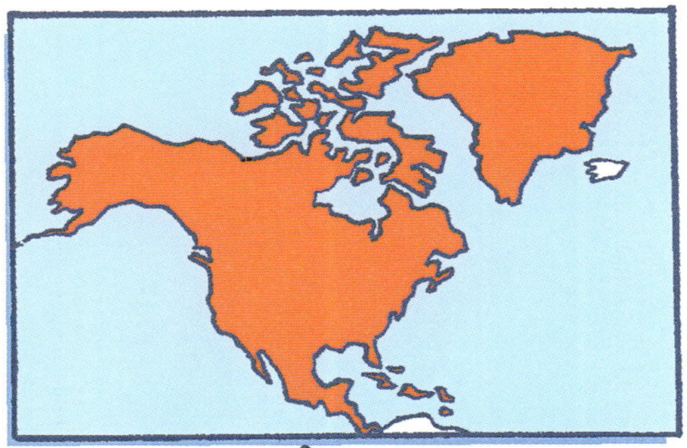

The continent of North America has high mountains, huge lakes and the tallest trees in the world.

It has big, busy cities too.

SOUTH AMERICA

Some of South America is covered in rainforest.

It has long rivers and ancient cities and temples.

OCEANIA

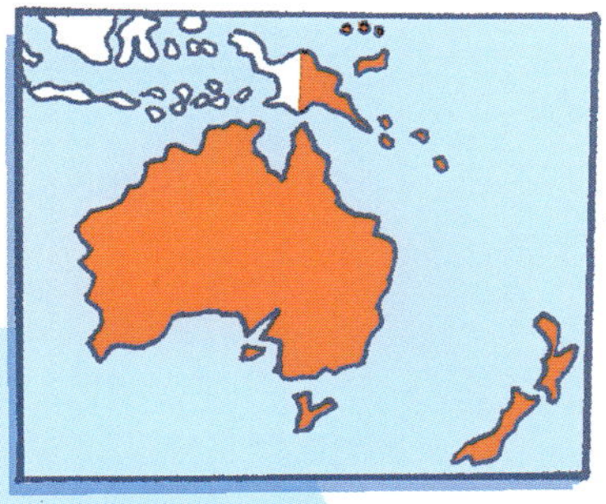

Oceania is made up of a lot of ISLANDS, surrounded by ocean.

There are forests, dusty deserts and sandy beaches.

ANTARCTICA

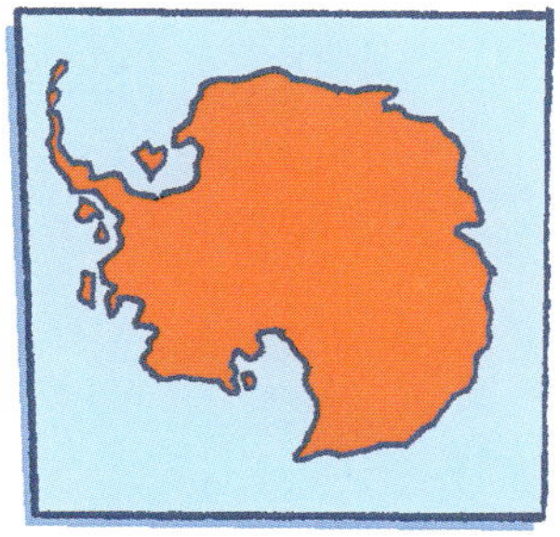

Antarctica is covered in ice.

It is the windiest place on Earth.

No one lives here all the time, except some animals.

Oceans

Earth's oceans are HUGE and SALTY.

ARCTIC OCEAN

This is the SMALLEST and COLDEST ocean. It covers the most northern part of the world.

PACIFIC OCEAN

This is the BIGGEST ocean. It covers more of the Earth than ALL the land put together.

ATLANTIC OCEAN

This is the second-biggest ocean. It covers a QUARTER of the Earth's surface.

INDIAN OCEAN

A lot of the water here is WARM. There are beautiful coral reefs.

SOUTHERN OCEAN

This surrounds Antarctica and is dotted with icebergs.

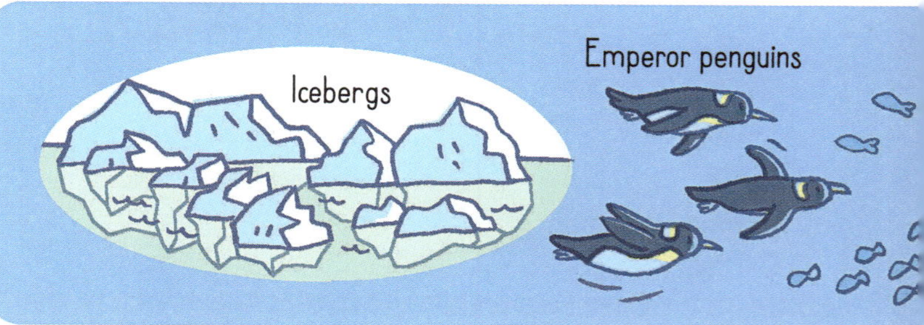

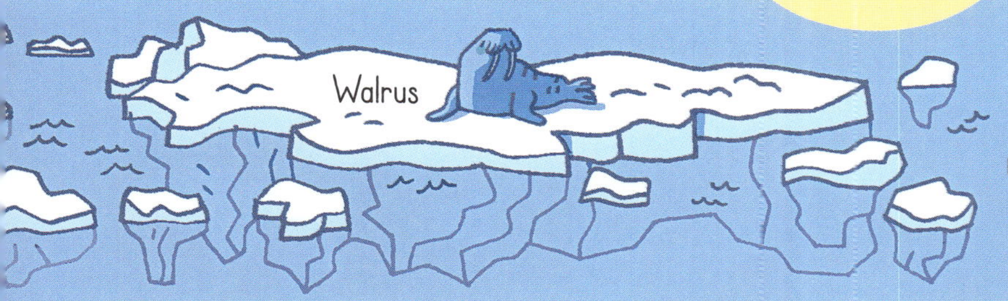

Far under the surface is the Mariana Trench. It's the DEEPEST place in the world.

The cold, choppy water is perfect for big groups of fish.

Mackerel

Halibut

Trees called MANGROVES grow out of the shallow ocean.

Mangroves

Whales travel thousands of miles to have their babies in the warm water.

Humpback whales

Blue whale

The ice-cold water is full of fish, and tiny creatures called krill that big whales gobble up.

Krill

Countries

The world's continents are divided up into lots of COUNTRIES.

Here's how the continent of South America is split up.

Each country has a FLAG...

...a **type** of **money**, called a CURRENCY...

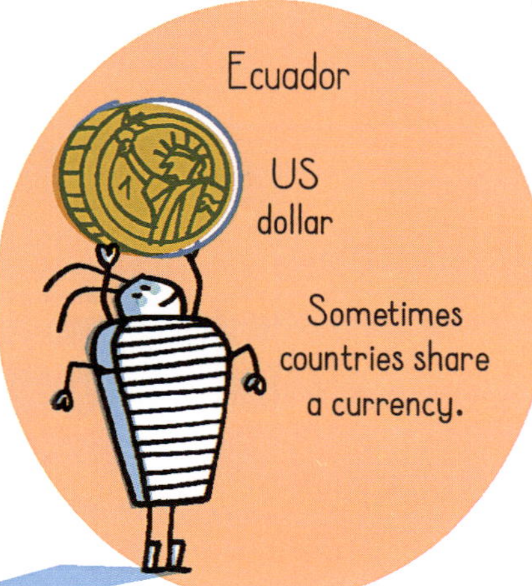

...and a LANGUAGE.

In some countries people speak more than one language,
and the same language can be spoken in lots of countries.

Ciao from Italy!
I have eaten lots of delicious pizza and pasta this week, and seen so many grand buildings.

I paid for my pizza with euros — luckily I can save any left over to spend in other parts of Europe.

From Dragonfly

Wow, I've explored SO many islands! The sea is warm and full of fish.

Everyone speaks Indonesian here, but there are over 700 other languages. Amazing!

Selamat tinggal (that means bye!)
Dragonfly

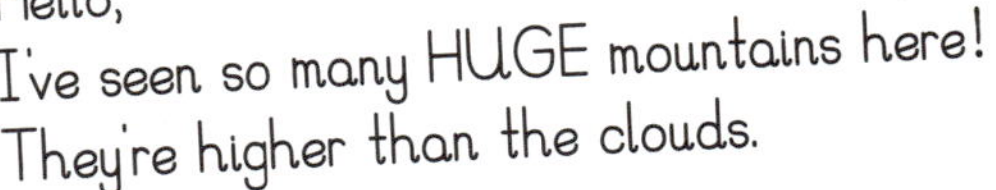

Hello,
I've seen so many HUGE mountains here! They're higher than the clouds.

Did you know that the flag of Nepal isn't a rectangle?

Until the next adventure,
Dragonfly

Every country has a **main** city called **the CAPITAL** city.
The capital city is **where** a **country's** rules and laws are **made.**

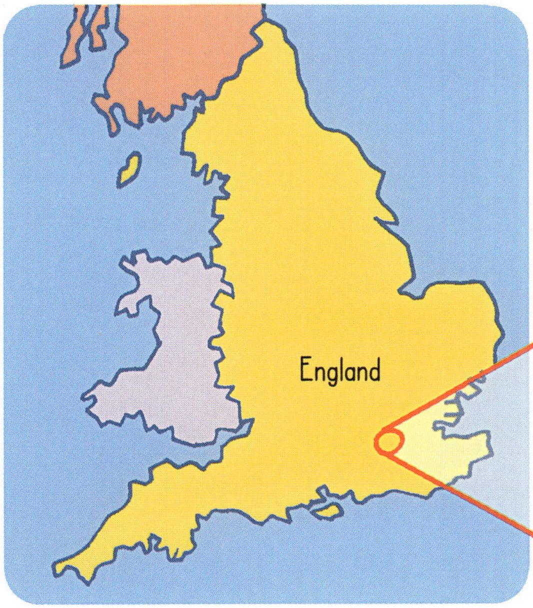

England

Capital cities often have old or important buildings, where the government is based.

London is the capital of England.

Sometimes the capital city is the biggest city, but not always.

You could make your own postcard for the country you live in.

People and places

Places people live in are called SETTLEMENTS.
They range from huge bustling cities to small quiet villages.

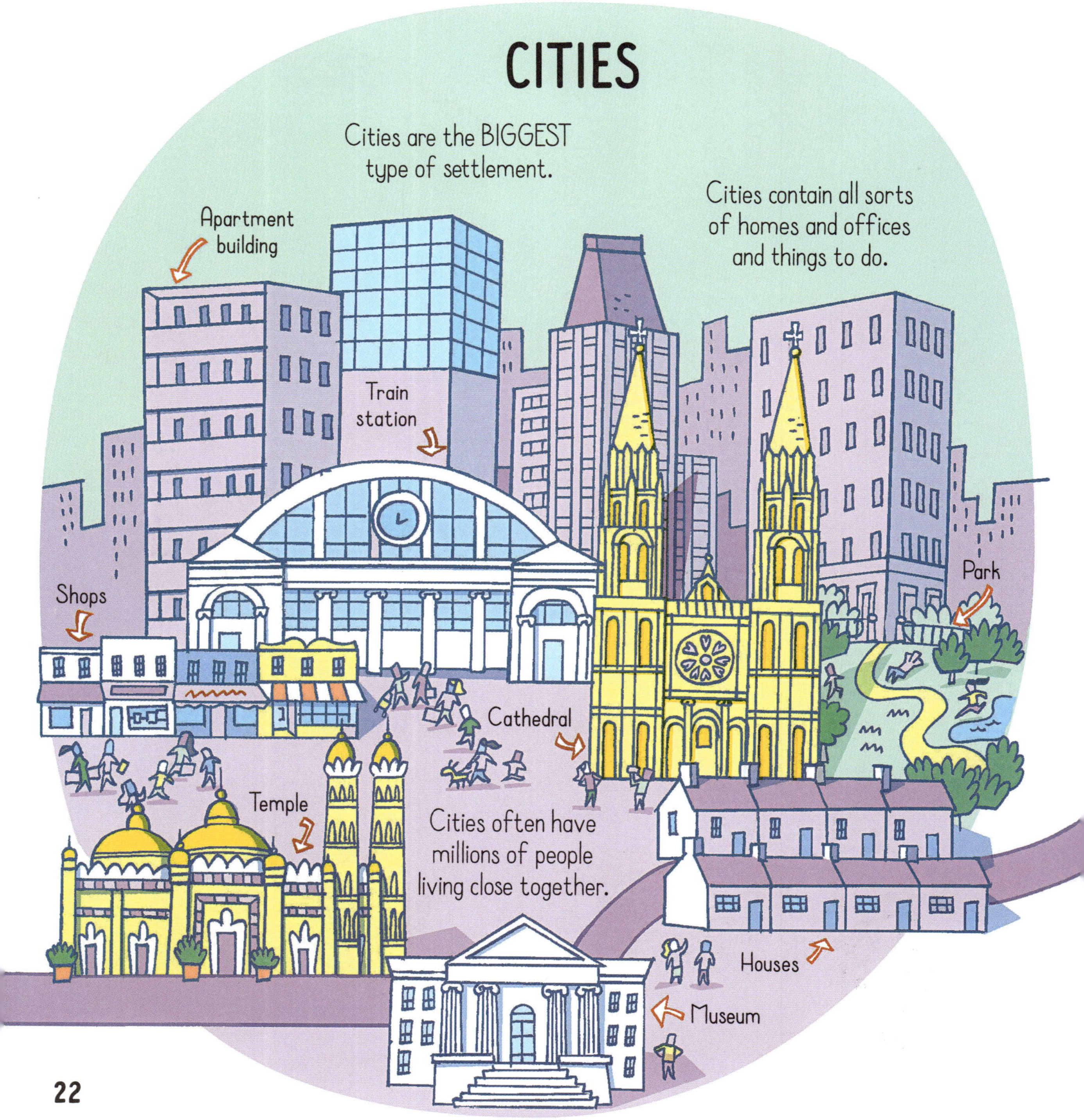

CITIES

Cities are the BIGGEST
type of settlement.

Cities contain all sorts
of homes and offices
and things to do.

TOWNS
Towns are smaller than cities, but still have everything people need.
School
Shops
Café
Towns usually have thousands of people.
VILLAGES
Villages cre very small sett ements.
Countryside
Shop
They usually have just a few hundred people.
Follow me to read about the countryside.

There aren't many buildings in the countryside,
but people often change the land in order to grow food.

FARMS

On this farm in the Netherlands,
rows and rows of the same
plants grow together.

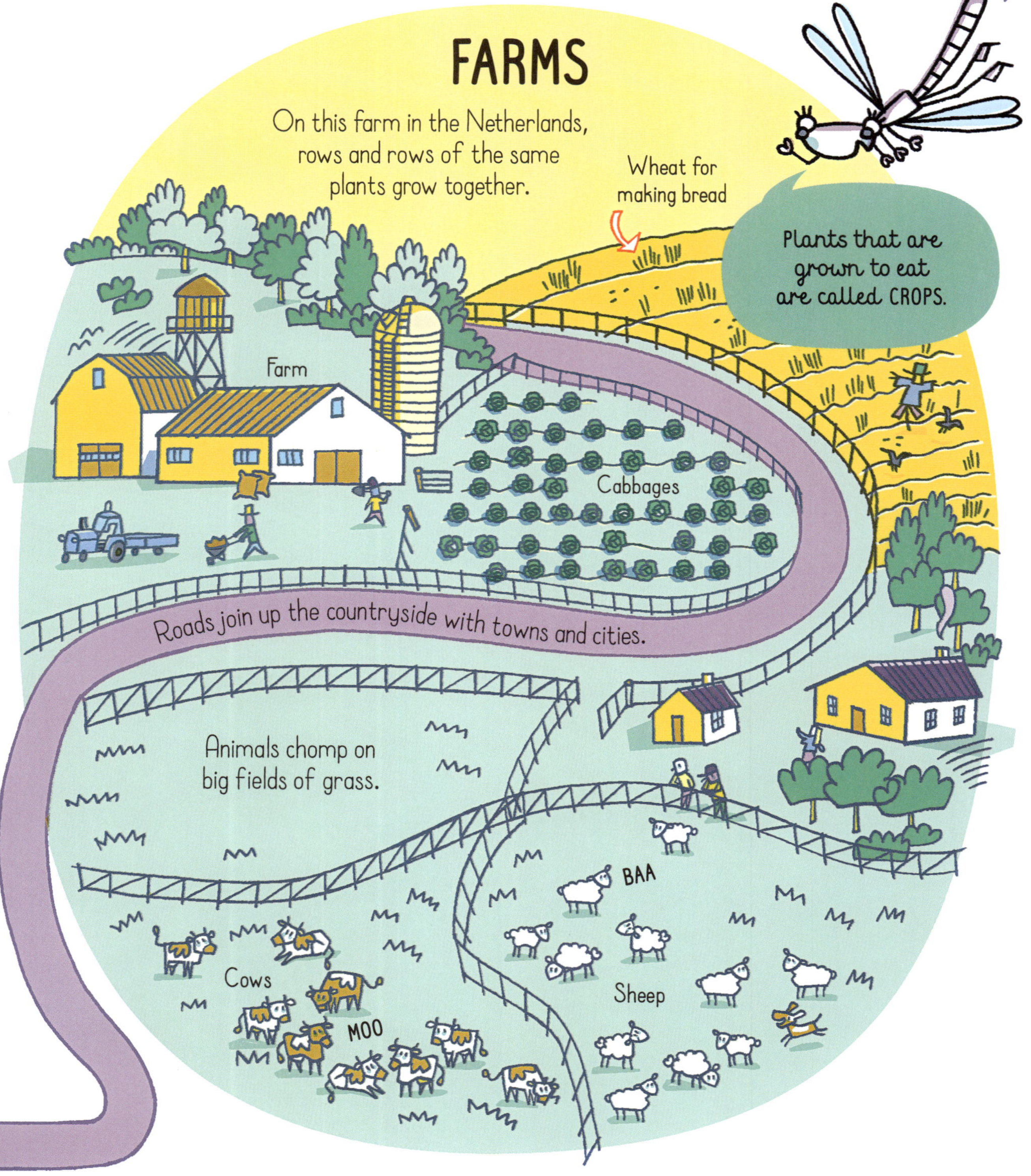

Different crops and animals are farmed in different parts of the world.

Settlements around the world are linked up by routes which criss-cross the land, sea and sky.

PLANE

Planes carry people across countries.

TRUCK

This truck full of food is on its way to a supermarket.

TRAIN

This train is carrying boxes of things made in factories...

SHIP

...to this ship, which will take them to countries around the world.

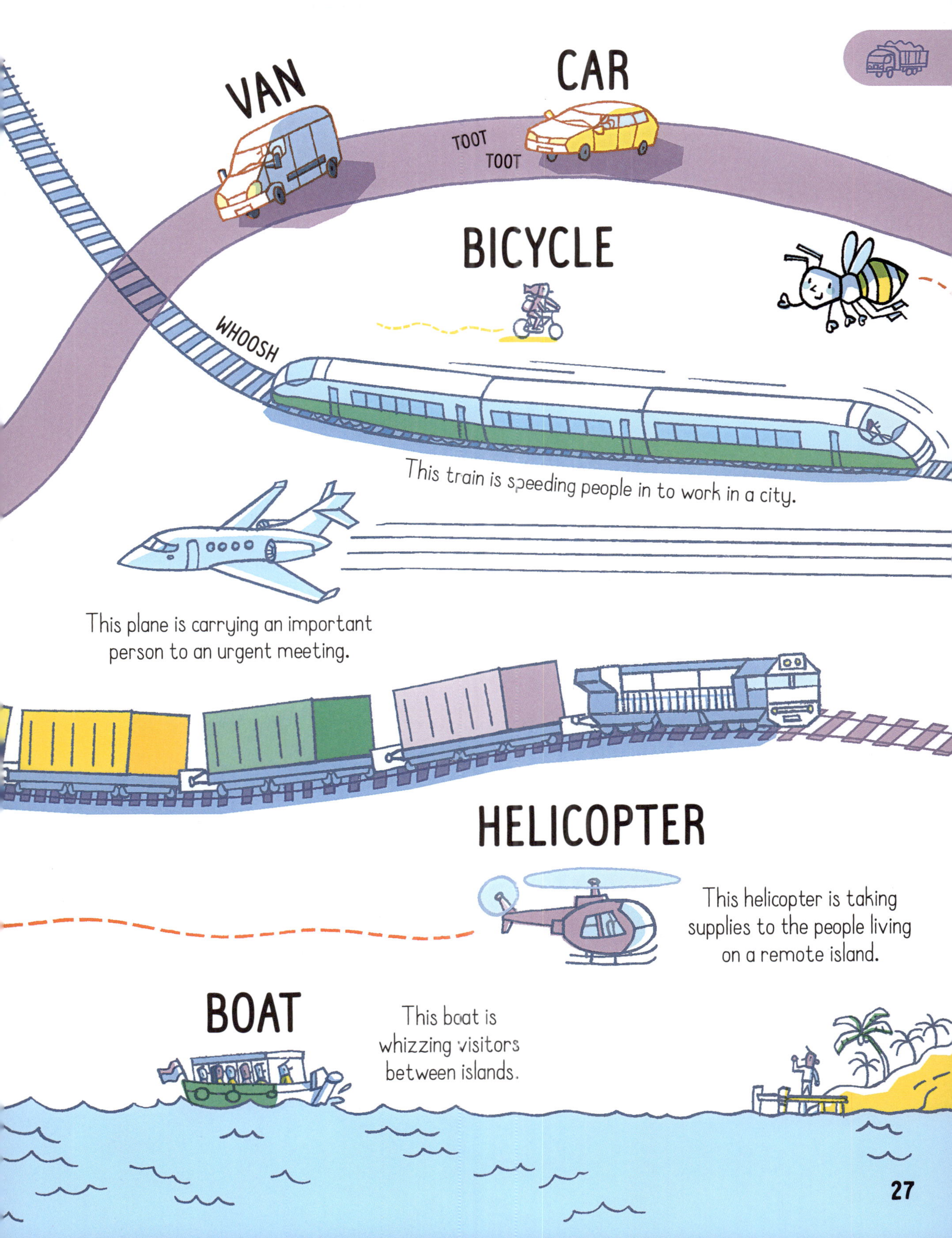

VAN
CAR
TOOT TOOT
BICYCLE
WHOOSH
This train is speeding people in to work in a city.
This plane is carrying an important person to an urgent meeting.
HELICOPTER
This helicopter is taking supplies to the people living on a remote island.
BOAT
This boat is whizzing visitors between islands.

Explore these pipes and tunnels to see what people have built UNDERGROUND.

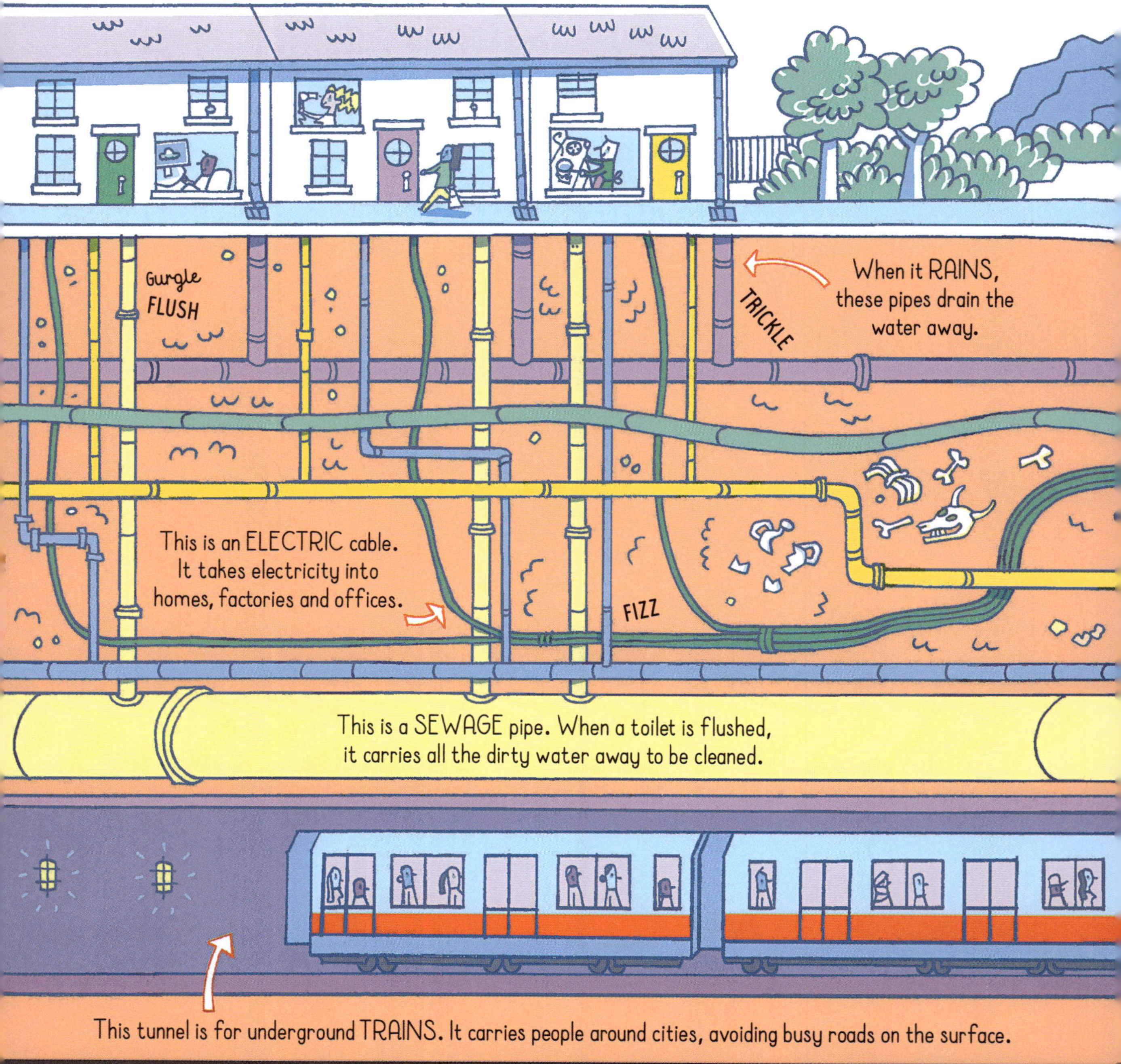

Gurgle
FLUSH

TRICKLE

When it RAINS, these pipes drain the water away.

This is an ELECTRIC cable. It takes electricity into homes, factories and offices.

FIZZ

This is a SEWAGE pipe. When a toilet is flushed, it carries all the dirty water away to be cleaned.

This tunnel is for underground TRAINS. It carries people around cities, avoiding busy roads on the surface.

Buried under the ground are all sorts of things that people dig up.

Clay

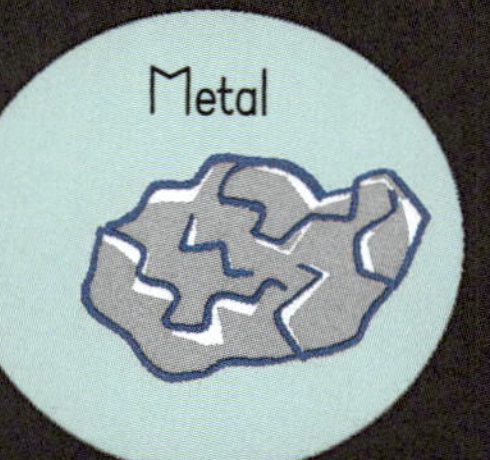

Metal

Precious stones

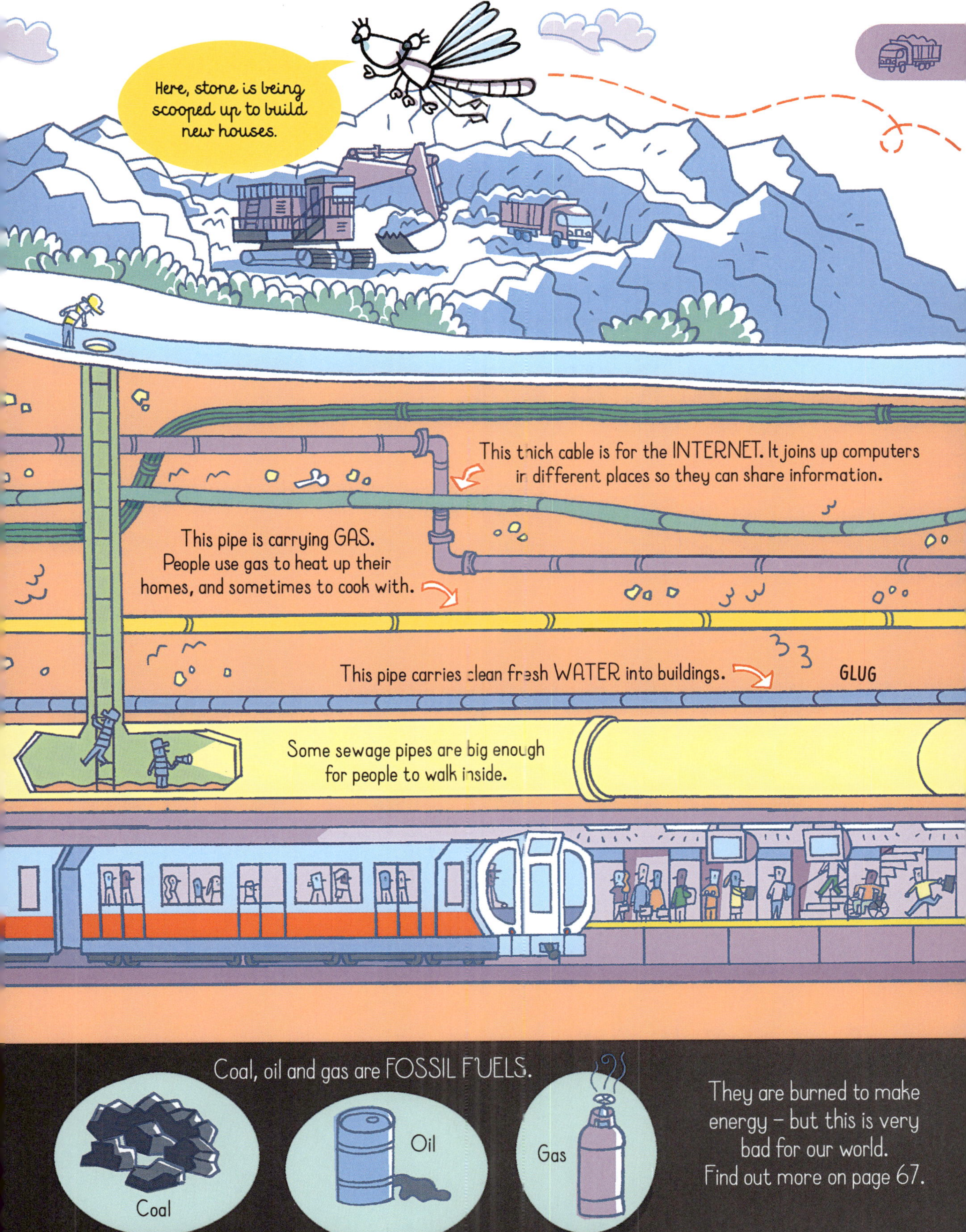

Here, stone is being scooped up to build new houses.
This thick cable is for the INTERNET. It joins up computers in different places so they can share information.
This pipe is carrying GAS. People use gas to heat up their homes, and sometimes to cook with.
This pipe carries clean fresh WATER into buildings.
GLUG
Some sewage pipes are big enough for people to walk inside.
Coal, oil and gas are FOSSIL FUELS.
Coal
Oil
Gas
They are burned to make energy – but this is very bad for our world. Find out more on page 67.

The natural world

The Earth is full of amazing NATURAL FEATURES.
Follow Dragonfly to discover some of them in
different places around the world.

**The first stop is KENYA, in east Africa.
What will Dragonfly find here?**

SAVANNAH

Savannahs are wide open spaces,
covered in grasses... and a few trees too.

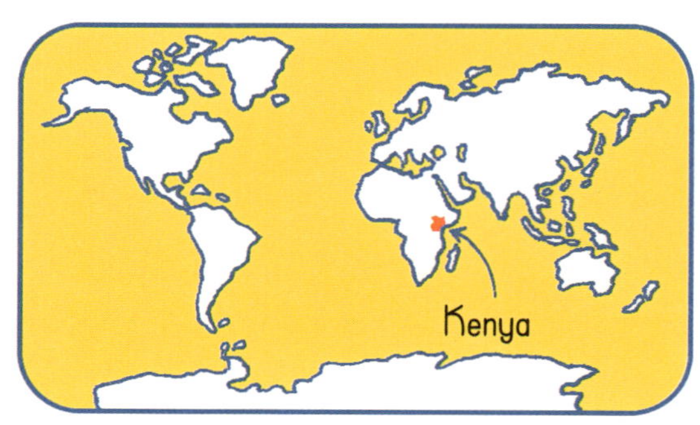

Baobab tree

They are home to
all sorts of amazing
big animals.

Giraffe

Acacia tree

Zebras

The thick trunk of a
baobab tree contains
a lot of water.

Elephants

Rhinoceros

DESERT

Deserts are DRY. This is the Nyiri desert in Kenya, and it is very hot.

There aren't many plants, and only a few animals.

It hardly ever rains in the desert. The only plants that grow are ones that don't need much water.

The next stop is VENEZUELA, in South America.
What natural features will Dragonfly see?
RAINFOREST
This is the Amazon RAINFOREST.
It's a hugely important place because it's
home to thousands of different living things.
Parrot
Sloth
YAWN
Troupial
Spider monkey
It RAINS nearly every day.
The rain keeps the trees
really green, and supports
lots of wildlife.
Anteater
Venezuela

WATERFALL

WATERFALLS are made by water wearing away rock, and making a sharp drop-off.

Water crashes over a ledge, and down into the river below.

Angel Falls in Venezuela is the world's HIGHEST waterfall!

Scarlet ibis

River dolphin

Kingfisher

RIVER

RIVERS weave through the forest. Eventually this one joins up to the Amazon River – one of the biggest rivers in the world.

Caiman

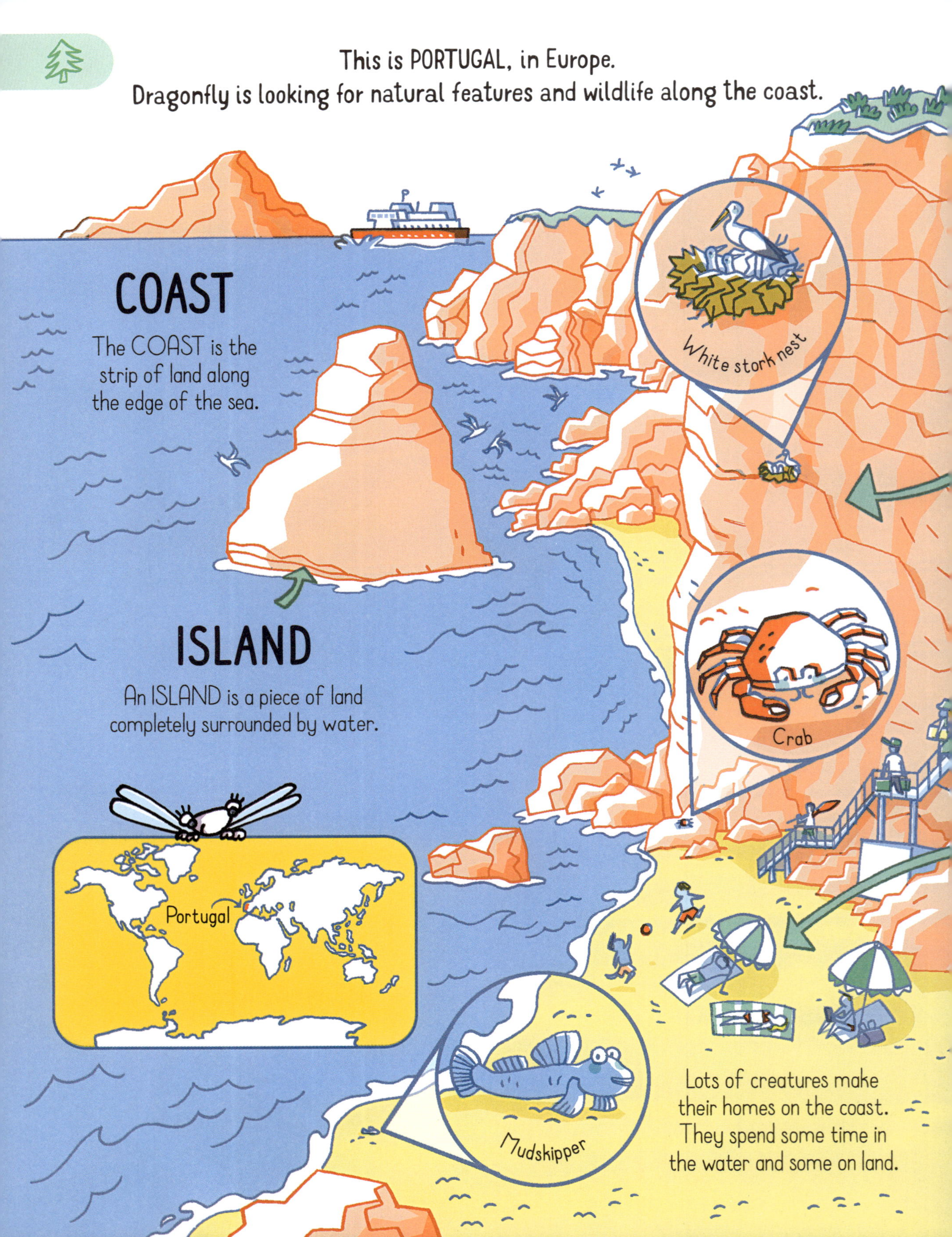

COAST

The COAST is the strip of land along the edge of the sea.

ISLAND

An ISLAND is a piece of land completely surrounded by water.

Lots of creatures make their homes on the coast. They spend some time in the water and some on land.

CLIFF

CLIFFS are tall, steep rocks where the land meets the sea.

When the sea crashes into a cliff, big rocks can break off and fall into the water.

Guillemots
Eggs
These birds live on the cliffs.

CREAK

SQUAWK
Gull

SPLASH!

The sea can wear away land very gradually or in big chunks. This is called EROSION.

BEACH

BEACHES start out as rocks. The sea hits the rocks and, over time, wears them down into...

...small PEBBLES

...and eventually SAND.

MOUNTAIN

These jagged MOUNTAINS
are made of hard rock.

Some trees can
grow straight
out of the rock.

In the winter,
everything was
covered in snow.

When the snow melts,
wild flowers bloom.

FJORD

This area of water is called a FJORD
(pronounced f-yord). It was made
when seawater flooded into an inlet
between the mountains.

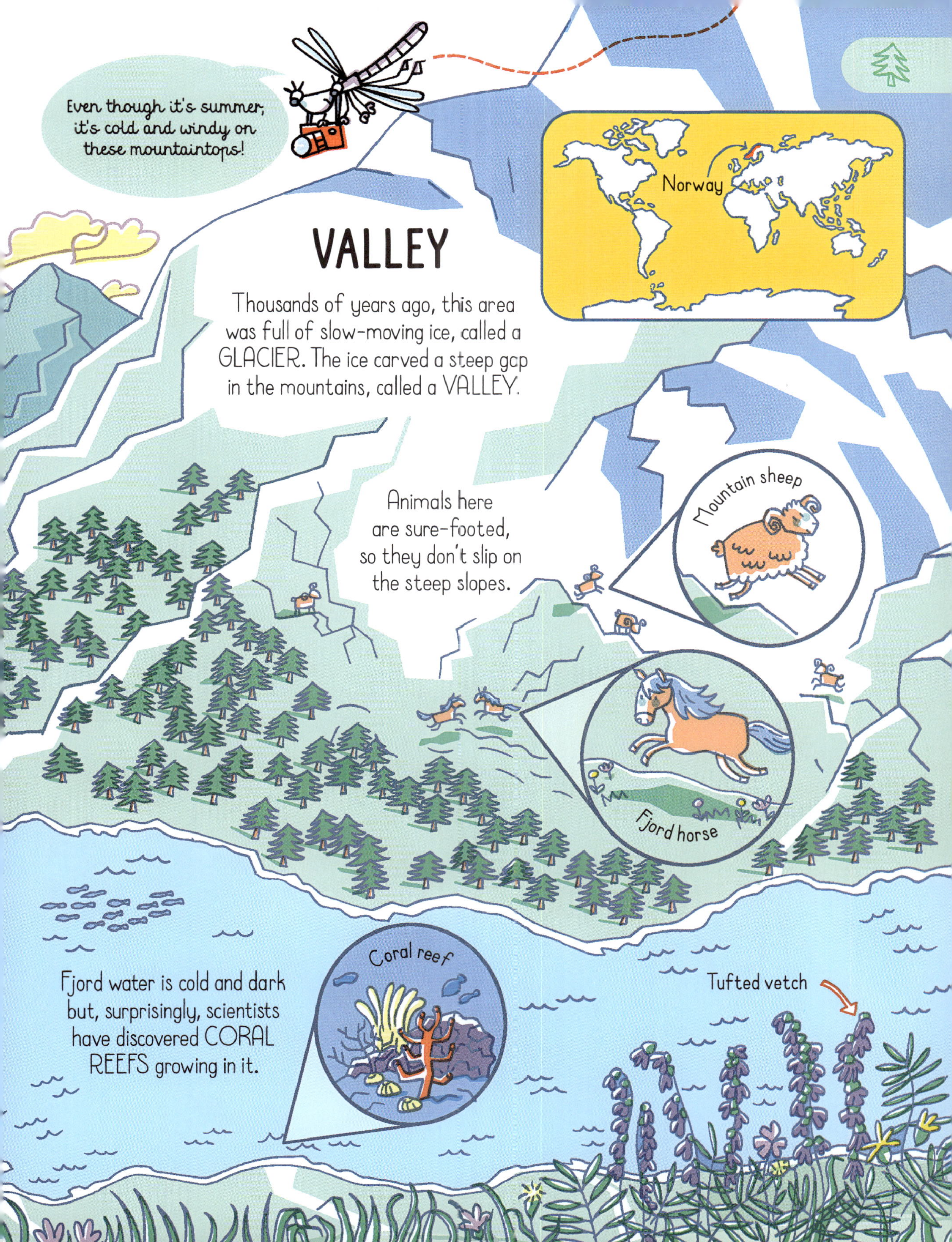

Even though it's summer, it's cold and windy on these mountaintops!
Norway
VALLEY
Thousands of years ago, this area was full of slow-moving ice, called a GLACIER. The ice carved a steep gap in the mountains, called a VALLEY.
Animals here are sure-footed, so they don't slip on the steep slopes.
Mountain sheep
Fjord horse
Fjord water is cold and dark but, surprisingly, scientists have discovered CORAL REEFS growing in it.
Coral reef
Tufted vetch

The last stop on our world tour is CANADA, in North America.
Let's see what natural features Dragonfly has found.

FOREST

This forest is made of EVERGREEN trees.
They are green even in the depths of winter.

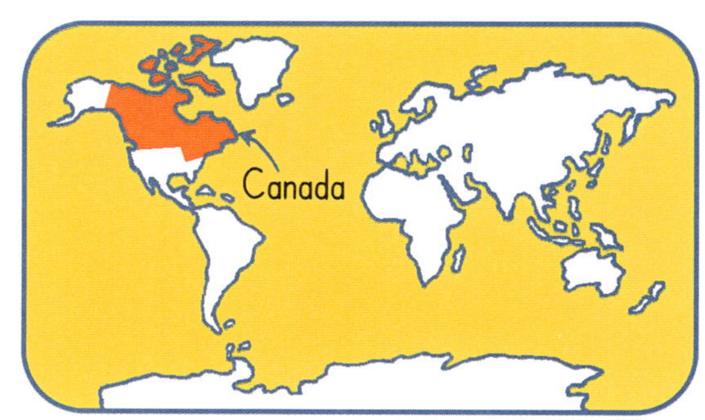

LAKE

This lake is nestled up in the mountains. As it's winter, it has frozen over.

HOT SPRING

Here, hot water bubbles up right out of the ground.

The hot water contains a substance called SULFUR, which makes it smell like rotten eggs.

What's the weather like?

Here are some kinds of weather.
They happen every day, somewhere in the world.

SUNSHINE

It can be sunny and hot,
or sunny and cold.

CLOUDS

Clouds are made of tiny water
drops or crystals of ice.

WIND

Wind is MOVING air.
Sometimes it's a
gentle breeze...

RAIN

Sometimes drops
of water from
clouds fall as rain.

HAILSTONES

Hailstones are chunks of ICE
that fall from clouds.

5mm (0.2 inches)

SNOW

When tiny ice crystals in clouds
stick together, they can make
SNOWFLAKES.

What the weather does in a particular place, day after day, year after year, is called the CLIMATE.

Different parts of the world have different climates.

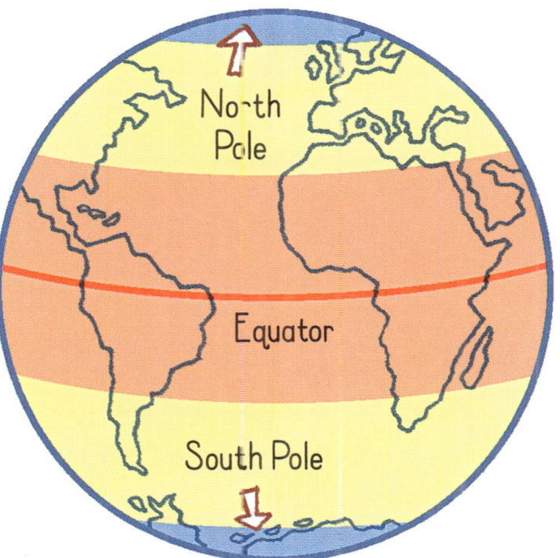

The POLES are COLD, as they are always furthest from the Sun. It hardly ever rains because it's too cold.

Around the middle of the Earth, at the EQUATOR, it's fairly warm all year round.

Between the poles and the equator, the climate is TEMPERATE.

That means cold winters...

...and warm summers.

Winter in Copenhagen, Denmark

Summer in Copenhagen, Denmark

Some places have FOUR seasons in a year.
These are usually places with a TEMPERATE climate.

SUMMER

It's warm and usually sunny.
Days are long.

AUTUMN
(OR FALL)

It gets cloudier and cooler,
and the days get shorter.

SPRING

The frost melts, the Sun comes
out and it's a little warmer.
Days get longer again.

WINTER

It's cold, dark and sometimes snowy.
The days are short.

Some places have just TWO seasons.
This is usually near the EQUATOR.

I live in Togo, near the equator in Africa.

DRY
This is the DRY season.
It's hot and sunny, and only rains occasionally.

This is actually the cooler of the two seasons.

Here, the days are the same length all year round.

WET
This is the WET, or RAINY, season.

It's EVEN hotter, but it rains a lot.

This lasts just over half the year.

Poland

SOUTH of the equator, July is in the winter.

Togo

In temperate regions NORTH of the equator, July is in the summer.

Dragonfly is off to explore some places in the world
with EXTREME weather, climates and seasons.

You'll get a warm welcome at Death Valley, in the USA.
It's one of the hottest places on Earth.

For several months a year in the north
of Finland, the Sun doesn't fully rise.

This shimmering glow
appears in the sky in winter.
It's called the NORTHERN LIGHTS.

This is the Democratic Republic of Congo, in Central Africa.

Lightning strikes here nearly every day!

It's extremely cold in Antarctica, and extremely dry too.

In some parts of Antarctica, it hasn't rained or snowed for over a million years.

In the same place in Finland, later in the year, for many months it never gets very dark.

It's the middle of the night!

YAWN!

I don't feel sleepy when it's so light!

Some of the most dramatic types of weather are STORMS.
A storm with thunder and lightning is known as a THUNDERSTORM.

STORM CLOUDS

These dark, low clouds are heavy with water droplets.

The droplets join together. They get bigger and bigger, and start to fall.

I knew a storm was coming because the sky turned SO DARK!

There's a FLASH of light, then a big RUMBLE.

LIGHTNING

LIGHTNING is a huge spark of electricity in the sky. The spark makes the air very hot.

This is FORKED lightning.

RUMBLE

THUNDER

The rumble is THUNDER. It's the noise of hot air exploding with a huge...

BOOM

CRACKLE

PLINK

SHEET lightning is when lightning flashes inside a cloud.

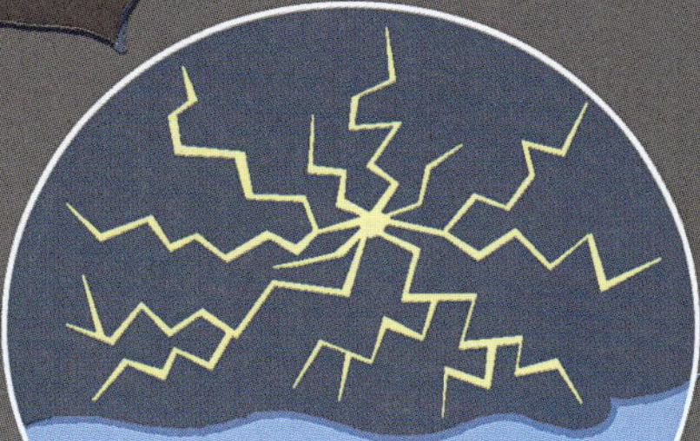

SPIDER lightning shoots in all directions.

You can tell how far away lightning is by counting the gap between seeing the flash and hearing the boom.

For every 3 seconds you count, the storm is 1km away. (Or for every 5 seconds you count, the storm is about 1 mile away.)

Some storms are even MORE EXTREME.

Volcanoes and earthquakes

Under your feet, the ground is MOVING. Most of the time it moves too slowly to notice. But sometimes, the effects are dramatic.

The Earth is covered by a thick, rocky CRUST. This crust is split into pieces, called PLATES.

The plates slot together like pieces of a puzzle.

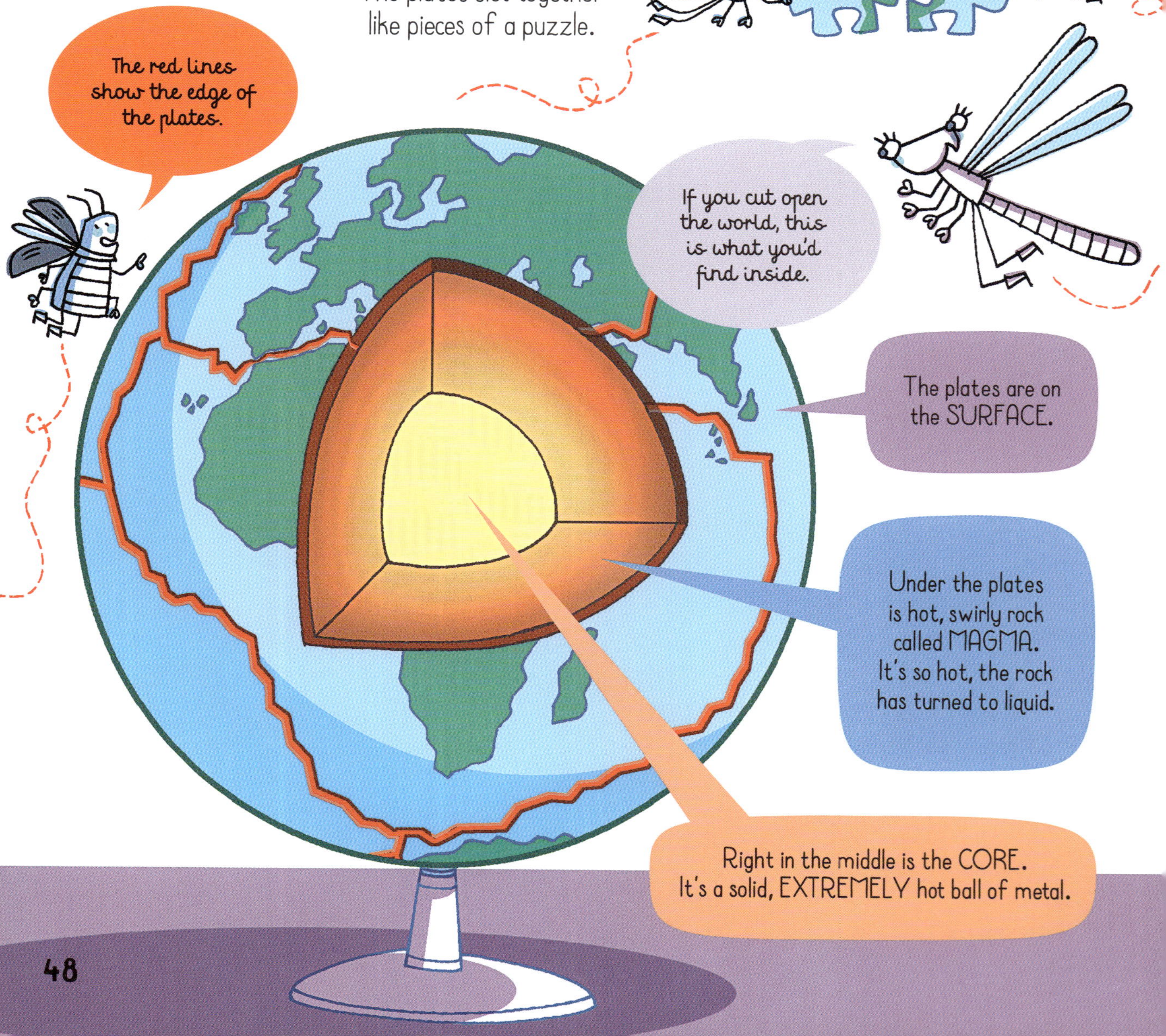

Ever so slowly, the plates are moving.
They move about 3-5cm (1-2 inches) every year.

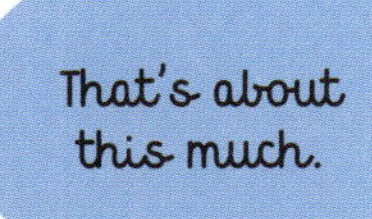

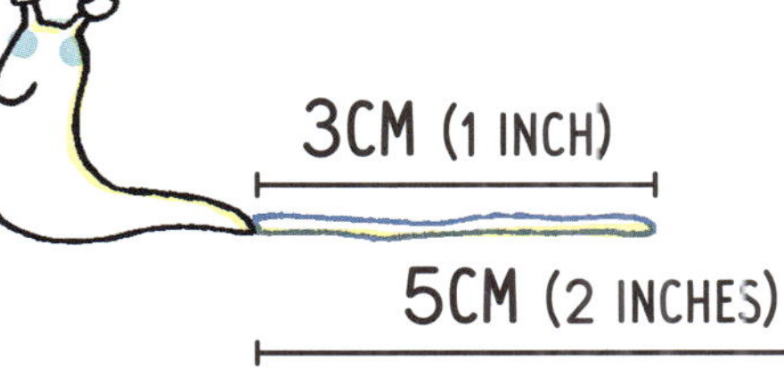

Where plates meet, those small movements can cause some BIG EFFECTS.

MOUNTAINS

When two plates push against each other, one can be forced up. This forms huge mountains.

SEA TRENCH

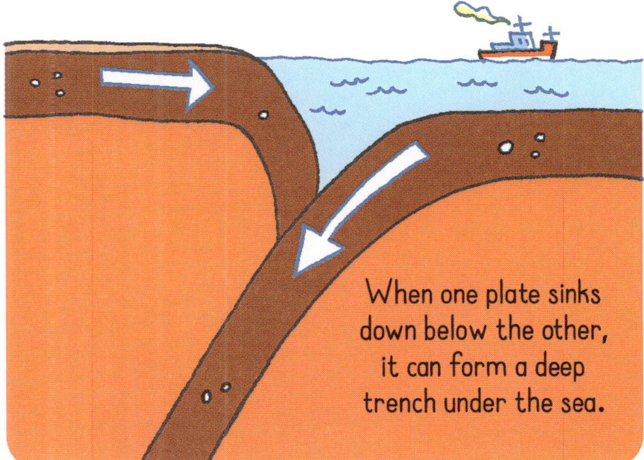

When one plate sinks down below the other, it can form a deep trench under the sea.

EARTHQUAKE

Sometimes plates rub against each other. This makes the ground rumble and shake, and can make the ground crack.

VOLCANO

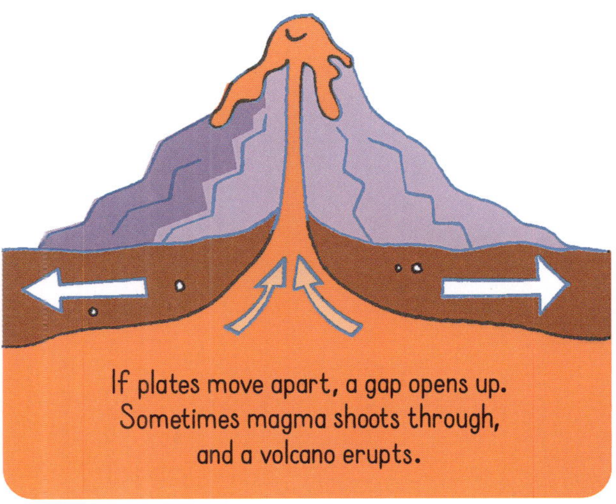

If plates move apart, a gap opens up. Sometimes magma shoots through, and a volcano erupts.

This volcano is ERUPTING!
Cough cough! Smoke and ash fill the sky.
KABOOM
When magma escapes and reaches the surface, it is called LAVA.
RUMBLE
TSSSS
The hot lava can move very quickly, burning everything it touches.
EVACUATE!
50

Most volcanoes are found where plates meet each other.

There are LOTS of volcanoes around the Pacific Ocean. There are so many here, it's known as the RING OF FIRE.

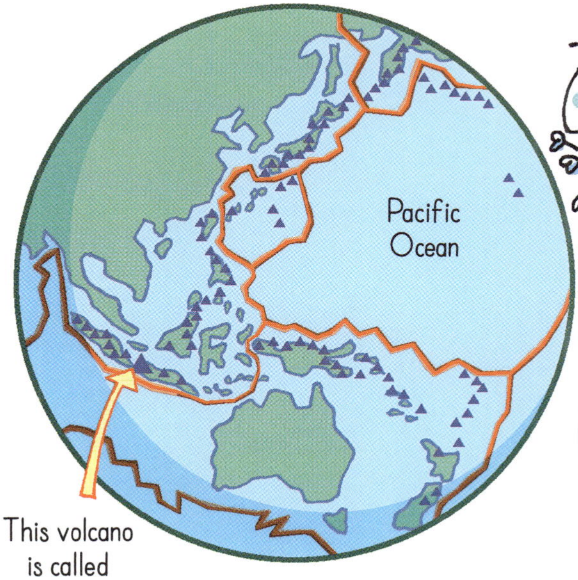

Krakatoa is in Indonesia. When it erupted in 1883, it sent up an ash cloud that made the WHOLE WORLD dark. People heard the eruption thousands of miles away.

There are three main kinds of volcanoes.

ACTIVE

ACTIVE volcanoes can erupt at any time. Scientists keep a close eye on them, so they can warn people if an eruption is coming.

DORMANT

DORMANT volcanoes might erupt ore day, but haven't for a long time. It's as if they're asleep.

EXTINCT

EXTINCT volcanoes erupted in the past, but won't ever erupt again. They're just hills or mountains now.

There's a rumble... a grumble... and the ground starts to SHAKE. It's an EARTHQUAKE!

Japan has more earthquakes than anywhere else in the world.

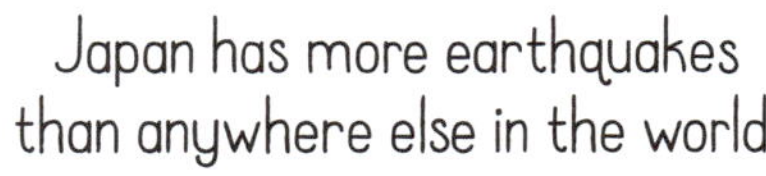

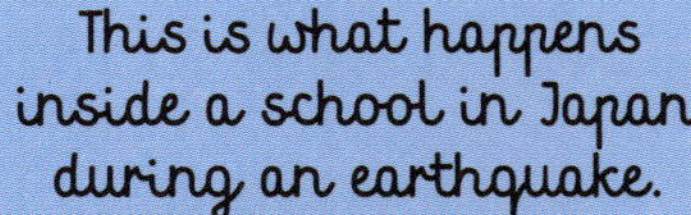

Everyone puts on special padded hoods to keep their heads safe.

The children get under their desks for protection.

When the shaking stops, everyone carries on with their day, safe and sound.

Earthquakes can happen whenever Earth's plates rub against each other.
There are over a THOUSAND earthquakes around the world every single day...
...but most of them are too small to notice.
In places that get a lot of earthquakes, buildings are designed to keep people safe when the ground shakes.
These skyscrapers are designed to sway...
...which helps them cope with the shock of an earthquake
Sometimes after an earthquake there are mini-quakes called AFTERSHOCKS. They can happen days, or even weeks later.
Oh no, not again!

If an earthquake happens under the ocean, it can cause huge waves of water. This is called a TSUNAMI.

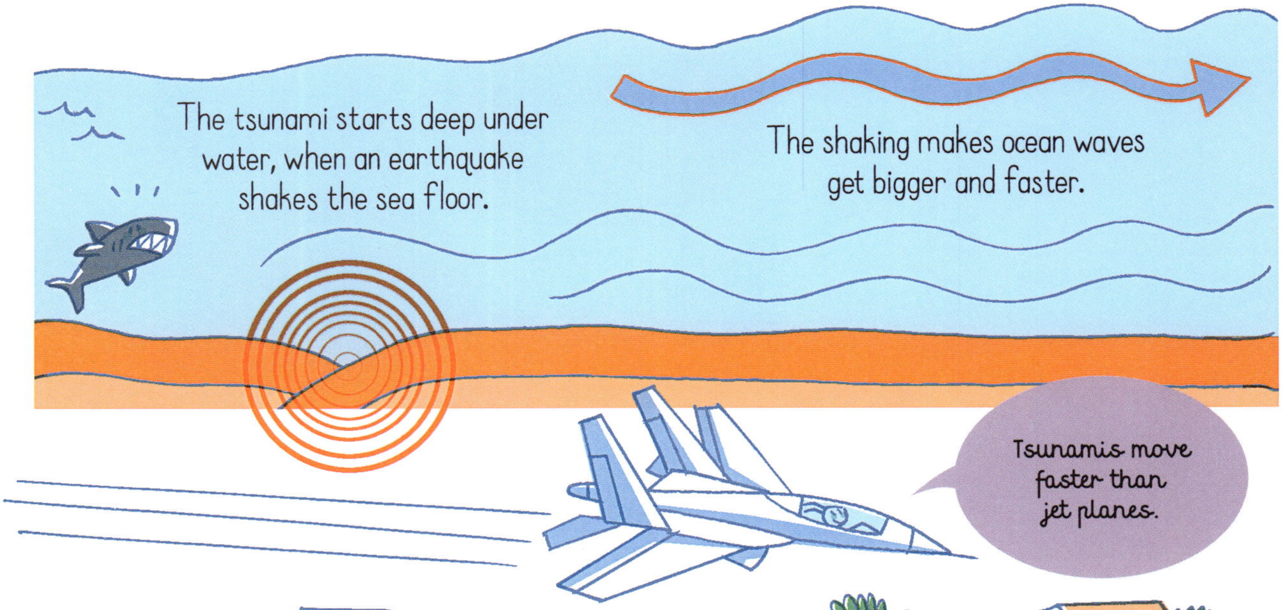

The tsunami starts deep under water, when an earthquake shakes the sea floor.

The shaking makes ocean waves get bigger and faster.

When the waves get to land, they keep on going. They are so powerful they can break trees and buildings.

To make sure people don't get hurt, scientists are always watching out for tsunamis.

This geyser is in Iceland. Boiling hot water bursts out and rushes high up into the air.

The word "geyser" comes from the name of this one, Geysir.

This jet of water is higher than a house.

There are LOTS of geysers, hot springs and volcanoes in Iceland, because it's where two plates meet.

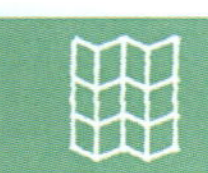

Mapping the world

People have made maps of everything from countries and continents to individual streets. Maps help us understand where things are in relation to everything else.

A GLOBE is really useful for seeing where continents, countries and oceans are.

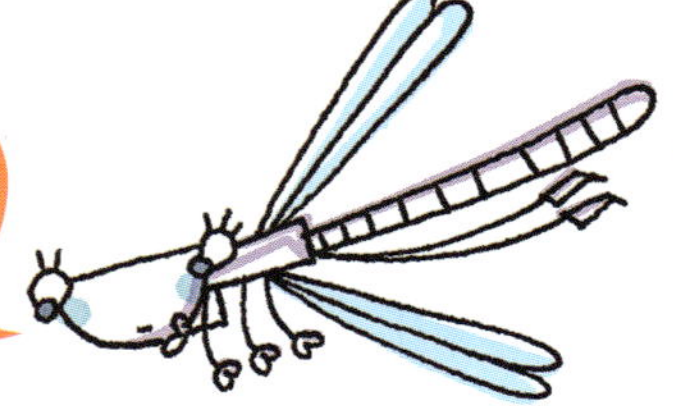

Globes are divided up by imaginary lines.

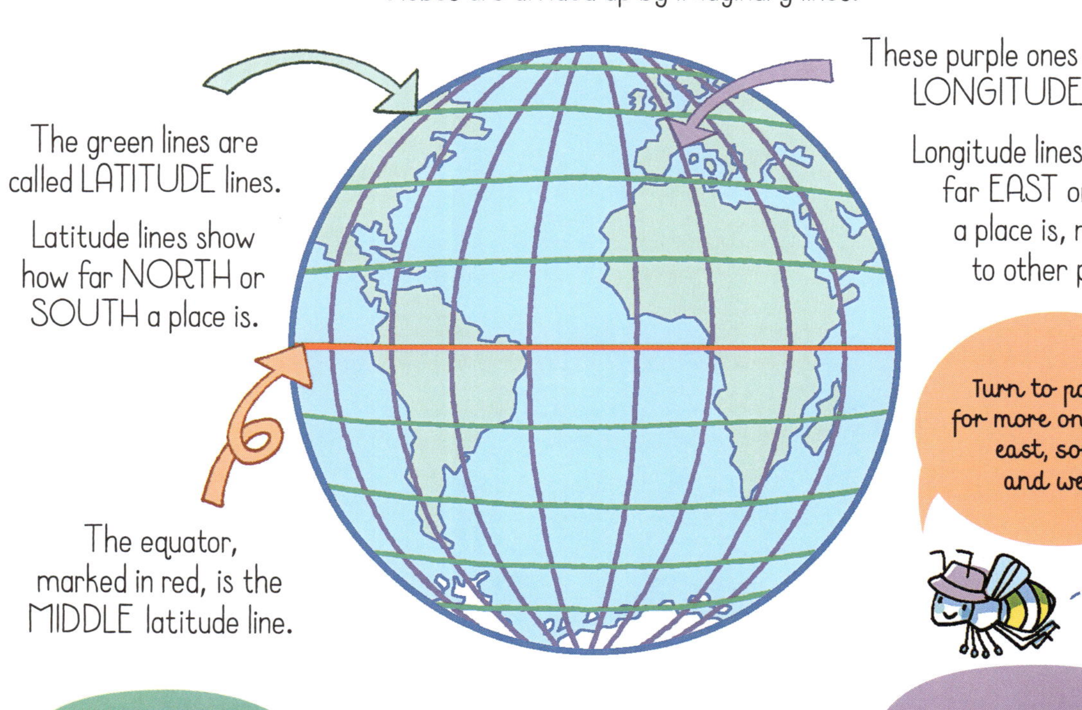

The green lines are called LATITUDE lines.

Latitude lines show how far NORTH or SOUTH a place is.

The equator, marked in red, is the MIDDLE latitude line.

These purple ones are called LONGITUDE lines.

Longitude lines show how far EAST or WEST a place is, relative to other places.

Turn to page 61 for more on north, east, south and west.

A MAP can show the whole world, one country, a city or just a small area of countryside.

Sometimes lots of maps are put together in a book called an ATLAS.

Maps are constantly being updated, as new roads and houses are built, and places change over time.

Map-makers use state-of-the-art technology to make sure maps are accurate.

Satellites zoom around Earth, taking photographs from space. The photographs help to make maps.

Ordnance Survey, who make maps of Great Britain, make 10,000 changes to their maps EVERY DAY.

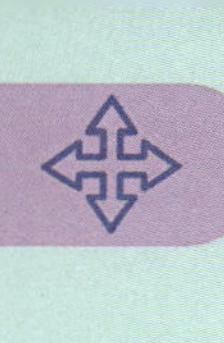

Finding your way

Maps are packed full of information. Once you know how to read them, they can tell you a lot about where you are and where you're going.

Maps use lines and symbols to show different things. Let's take a look at what they mean...

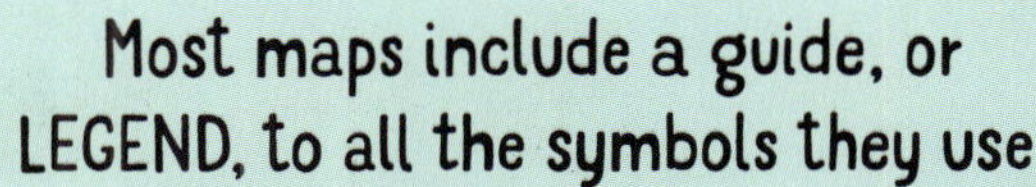

Most maps include a guide, or LEGEND, to all the symbols they use.

Look at the legend below.
Can you spot all the symbols on the map?

 Cycleway

 Campsite

 Parking

 Hospital

 Viewpoint or lookout

 Swimming pool

 Fuel

 Picnic area

 Footpath or trail

To find your way using a map, there are a few extra things it's useful to know about.

SCALE

Maps have to shrink what they show – otherwise they'd be far too big to carry. A map's SCALE tells you how much it's been shrunk.

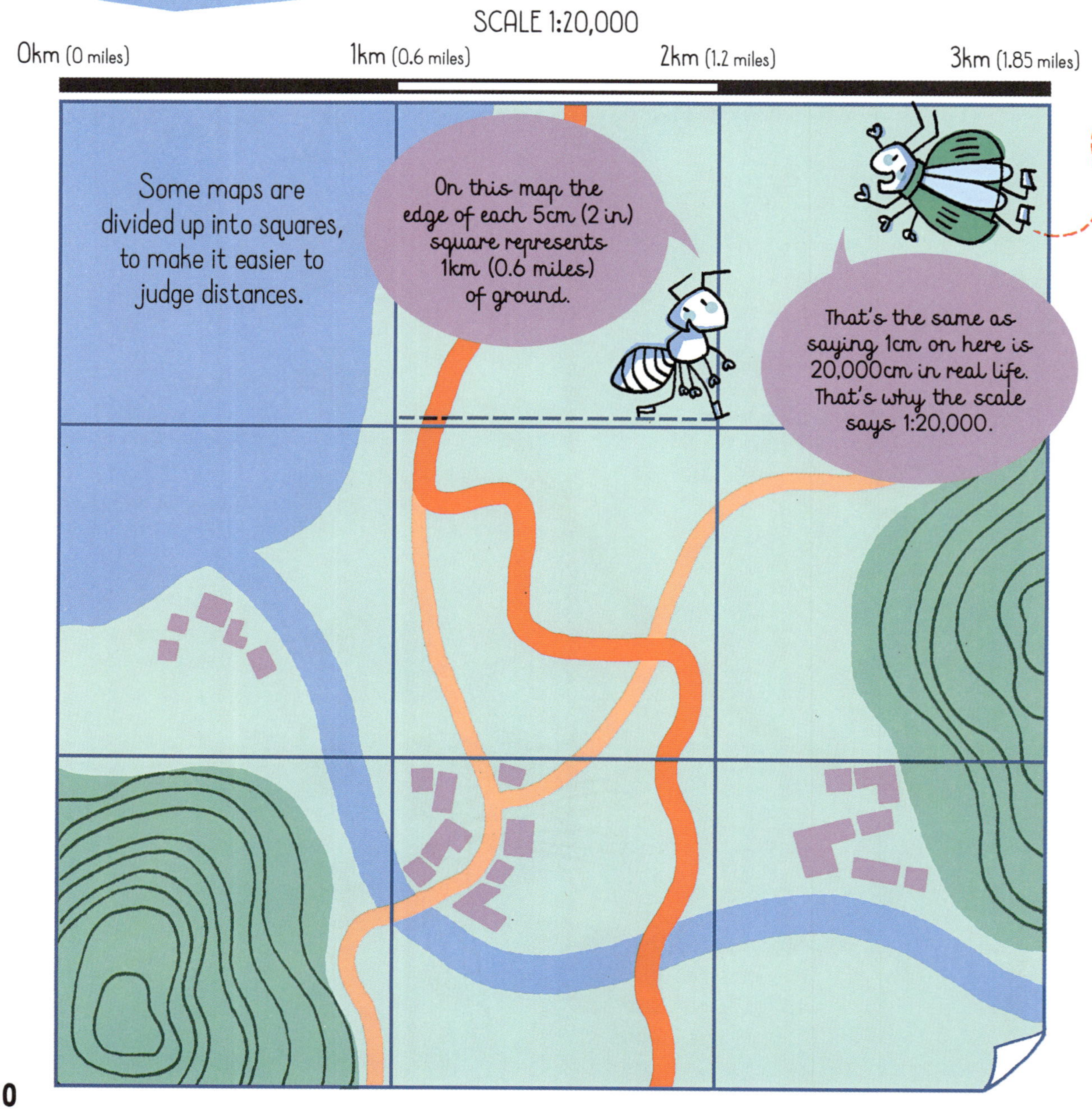

SCALE 1:20,000

0km (0 miles) 1km (0.6 miles) 2km (1.2 miles) 3km (1.85 miles)

DIRECTIONS

These are the four main directions.

Where do you live?

Everything from buildings and landscapes, to weather and climate, makes up the place where you live.

These bugs are describing the places they live.
Match them up with the pictures below – who lives where?

Where do YOU live? What's it like there?
Use the questions below to help you describe it.

Which
COUNTRY
do you live in?

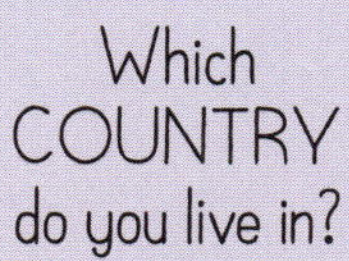

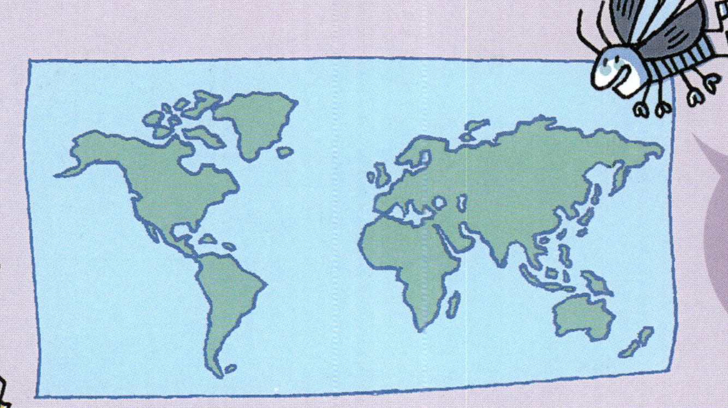

You can look
back through
the book to help
you answer the
questions!

How many seasons do you have?
What's the weather like?

What kind of
SETTLEMENT
do you live in?

A house in the
countryside?

A village?

A city?

A town?

Make a poster to tell people
about where you live. Start with
the answers to these questions,
and add some pictures.

Mountains?

What natural
features are
there nearby?

The sea?

A river?

Hills?

WEATHER

Keep a diary of the weather where you live,
for a whole week. Was it dry, rainy, hot or cold?
Did the weather change every day?

You can measure how much rain falls by making your own rain gauge, like this.

Carefully cut the top
off an old plastic bottle.
You can ask a grown up
to help with this part.

Turn the top
upside down.
Place it inside the
bottle like a funnel.

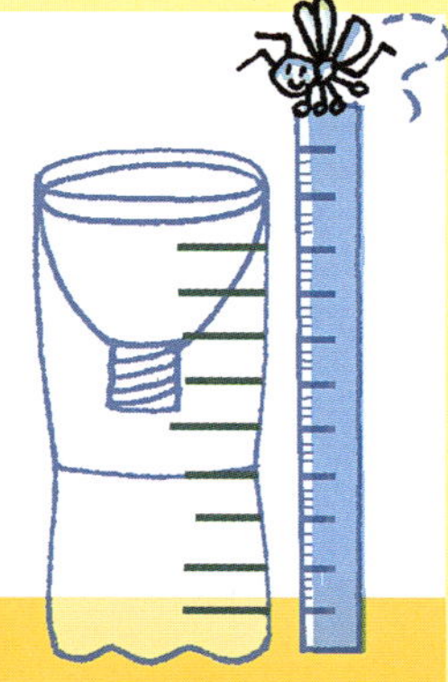

Hold a ruler against
the bottle and mark
on cms or inches.

Put it outside and wait
for the rain! Use your
markings to see how
much rain has fallen.

WILDLIFE

How many birds can you spot while you're out and about?
You could look on just one day, or keep a tally over a week.

You might see different birds!

You could do a tally for other types of animals too.

Pigeon

Blue jay

Sparrow

Duck

MAPS

Try drawing a simple map of your road, and the area around it.

Looking after our world

Our world is full of beautiful and amazing things. But it all needs looking after, or it won't stay beautiful forever.

Here are some of the things that Dragonfly has seen on her travels, which put parts of our world in danger.

PLASTIC EVERYWHERE

When people throw away plastic, some of it ends up in the sea. This can hurt sea life.

NOT ENOUGH TREES

Trees help to keep the air clean, and are home to many animals. But every day forests get smaller.

LOTS OF WASTE

There are seven billion people on Earth, throwing things away every day. All that waste is piling up.

TOO HOT!

When coal and oil are burned to make electricity, they pump out a gas called carbon dioxide.

This gas covers the Earth like a blanket. Each year the world gets a little hotter.

MELTING ICE

As the world warms up, ice at the poles melts. Animals there are struggling to survive.

ANIMALS IN DANGER

When trees are cut down, and the climate warms up, animals lose their food and homes.

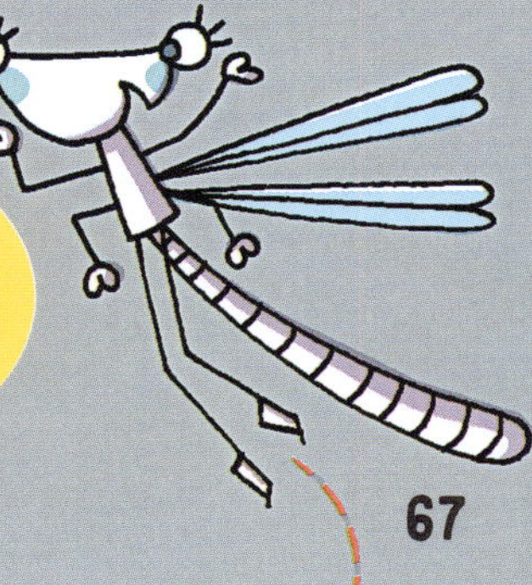

I'm looking at different plants, to see how they cope with a changing climate.

I build solar panels. They make electricity from the Sun, without creating pollution.

We are creating a new national park.

No one can chop down trees or build houses in the park...

LEAFY PARK
OPENING TODAY

...so it will help protect all the wildlife that lives here.

I study rare birds, to learn how to protect them.

I'm putting forward a new LAW to use more eco-friendly electricity.

We're making a TV show to tell people what's happening to wildlife.
I keep track of how many fish live here. I'll warn people if numbers drop. 
SAVE OUR PLANET 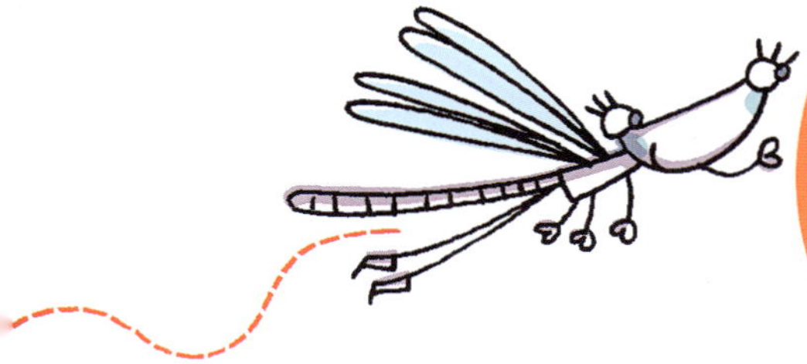 
I'm asking governments to take climate change seriously.
I come down to the beach every day to pick up plastic. 
I'm making places for bugs to live in my garden! 
Long grass
Bee-friendly flowers
Logs to make a bug home

WORLD HELPER GUIDE

SAVE WATER

Take a shower instead of a bath. Saving water is really good for the environment!

You could collect rainwater to water your plants.

SAVE ENERGY

Turn off the light as you leave a room, to use less electricity.

If you feel chilly, put on an extra layer rather than turning up the heating.

CUT DOWN POLLUTION

To cut down the number of polluting vehicles on the roads, walk or cycle when you can...

Plant some flower seeds. As they grow they absorb carbon dioxide, and bees love them too.

To save things just being thrown away, try to:

REDUCE

Use LESS!

Buy fewer new things, if you don't really need them.

REUSE

Use things again...

...or use them in a new and different way.

RECYCLE

When you've finished with something, recycle it so it can be turned into something NEW.

Give away or sell things you don't need any more, rather than throwing them away.

When you can, buy things second hand rather than new, so less stuff ends up as waste.

Tell other people everything you know about looking after the world.

Everyone together

We can all make a difference to the world around us.
Here are some suggestions.

Respect EVERYBODY.

Look after the world around you.

Care for all living things.

Help at home.

Try to be helpful in your community.

Everyone on Earth is a CITIZEN of our world. Being a GREAT citizen means caring for the planet...
...AND for other people.

...whatever their beliefs
...and however they live their life.

Take your litter home with you.
Respect nature – don't pick plants or disturb wildlife.

Follow rules that keep everyone safe.
Be kind to people who need more time or help.

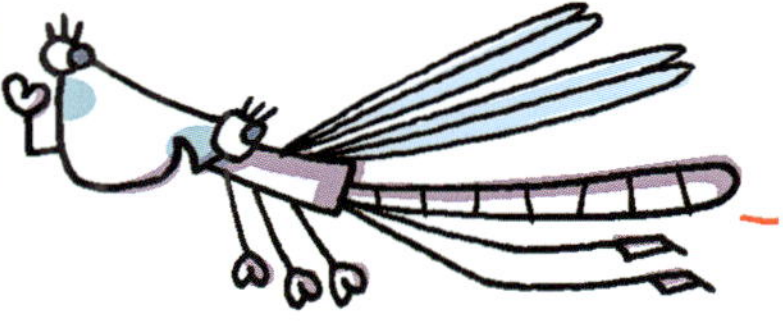

Together we can make our planet a happier and healthier place for everyone to enjoy.

Countries of the world

Here are all the countries mentioned in this book.
Each country is shown beside its flag. You'll also see its capital city,
and the page (or pages) where you can read about it.

ARGENTINA
Buenos Aires
pages 18-19

CHILE
Santiago
page 18

AUSTRALIA
Canberra
page 15

CHINA
Beijing
page 12

BOLIVIA
Sucre, La Paz
page 18

COLOMBIA
Bogotá
page 18

BRAZIL
Brasilia
pages 18-19, 25

**DEMOCRATIC REPUBLIC
OF THE CONGO**
Kinshasa
page 45

CANADA
Ottawa
pages 38-39

DENMARK
Copenhagen
page 41

ECUADOR
Quito
pages 18-19

GUYANA
Georgetown
page 18

EGYPT
Cairo
page 13

ICELAND
Reykjavik
page 55

ETHIOPIA
Addis Ababa
page 25

INDIA
New Delhi
page 12

FINLAND
Helsinki
pages 44-45

INDONESIA
Jakarta
pages 20, 51

FRANCE
Paris
pages 13, 57

ITALY
Rome
page 20

GERMANY
Berlin
page 19

JAMAICA
Kingston
page 63

GREECE
Athens
page 13

JAPAN
Tokyo
page 52

NEW ZEALAND
Wellington
page 25

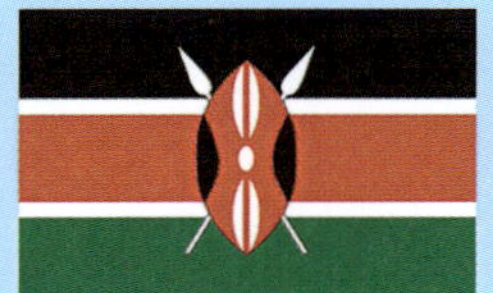
KENYA
Nairobi
page 30

NORWAY
Oslo
pages 36-37

MALI
Bamako
page 25

PAKISTAN
Islamabad
page 62

MEXICO
Mexico City
page 62

PARAGUAY
Asunción
page 18

MOROCCO
Rabat
page 62

PERU
Lima
pages 14, 18

NEPAL
Kathmandu
page 20

POLAND
Warsaw
page 42

THE NETHERLANDS
Amsterdam, The Hague
page 24

PORTUGAL
Lisbon
pages 19, 34-35

RUSSIA
Moscow
page 25

THAILAND
Bangkok
page 25

SAMOA
Apia
page 16

TOGO
Lomé
page 43

SOUTH AFRICA
Cape Town, Pretoria, Bloemfontein
page 21

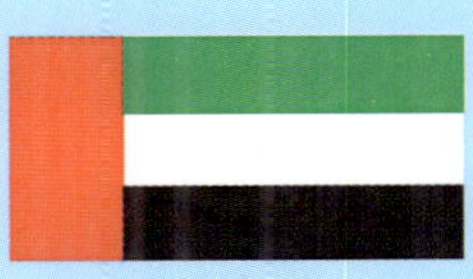
UNITED ARAB EMIRATES
Abu Dhabi
page 62

SOUTH KOREA
Seoul
page 12

UNITED KINGDOM
London
pages 21, 57

SPAIN
Madrid
pages 19, 25

UNITED STATES OF AMERICA
Washington DC
pages 14, 16, 44

SURINAME
Paramaribo
page 18

URUGUAY
Montevideo
page 18

SWEDEN
Stockholm
page 13

VENEZUELA
Caracas
pages 18, 32

Glossary

Atlas – a book of maps

Capital city – the main city where a country's rules are made

Climate – the weather across the year in a certain place, year after year

Climate crisis – the big and bad effects of the Earth getting hotter

Coast – where the land meets the sea

Continents – the seven main areas of land on the planet

Contours – lines on a map that show how high the land is

Coral reef – a ridge of rock under the sea, with coral living all over it, and home to lots of creatures

Currency – the type of money used in a country

Data – another word for information

Earthquake – a huge shaking of the ground, when the Earth's plates rub together

Equator – an imaginary line around the middle of the Earth

Fieldwork – going out to collect information

Fossil fuels – coal, oil and gas, which are burned to make electricity

Geography – the study of our world

Geyser – a place where hot water shoots high out of the ground

Glacier – a slow-moving river of ice

Globe – a small, round model of the Earth

Government – the group of people in charge of a country

Hot spring – a place where hot water bubbles out of the ground

Hurricane – a huge swirling storm that forms over warm seas

Latitude – imaginary horizontal lines that run around the Earth, and are used to describe how far north or south somewhere is

Lava – hot rock that has erupted out of a volcano

Longitude – imaginary vertical lines that run from pole to pole, and are used to describe how far east or west a place is

Magma – hot, liquid rock under the Earth's surface

Map – a picture that shows where things are in relation to other things

Plates – the huge pieces that make up the crust over the surface of the Earth

Poles – the places furthest north and south on the planet

Recycling – turning something old into something new to be used again

Scale – how much the things on a map are shrunk by

Seasons – periods of different weather through the year

Settlement – a place where people live, including cities, towns and villages

Temperate – a climate with warm summers and cold winters

Tsunami – a rush of water caused by an earthquake under the sea

Valley – a steep-sided gap in mountains, worn away by water or ice

Volcano – an opening in the Earth's crust where magma can erupt

Index

A

Africa 11, 13, 30-31, 43, 45
Antarctica 10-11, 15, 16, 45
Arctic Ocean 10-11, 16-17
Asia 11, 12
Atlantic Ocean 10-11, 16-17
atlases 56-57

C

cities 12, 13, 21, 22, 62, 63
coral reefs 16, 37
countries 18-21

D

data 7, 64
deserts 13, 15, 31, 62

E

earthquakes 48, 49, 52-53, 54
electricity 28, 46, 67, 70
equator 6, 41, 43, 56
Europe 11, 13, 20, 34-35, 36-37, 42

F

farms 24-25, 66
flags 19, 20, 74-77
forests 15, 38, 66
fossil fuels 29

G

geysers 55
globes 6, 56-57
governments 18, 69

I

ice 8, 15, 16, 17, 37, 40, 67
Indian Ocean 11, 16-17
islands 15, 16, 34

L

lakes 14, 39
languages 19, 20

M

maps 6, 10-11, 56-61, 65
mountains 5, 20, 36-37, 39, 49, 51, 62

N

natural features 30-39, 63
North America 10, 14, 38-39

O

Oceania 11, 15
oceans 10-11, 16-17

P

Pacific Ocean 10-11, 16-17, 51
plastic 66, 68, 69
plates 48-49, 51, 53
poles 6, 10-11, 16, 41, 44, 67

R

rainforests 14, 32-33
recycling 71
rivers 14, 33, 58

S

seasons 42-43, 44-45, 63
South America 10, 14, 18, 32-33
Southern Ocean 10-11, 16-17
storms 5, 46-47

T

trains 26-27, 28-29
tsunamis 54

V

volcanoes 48, 49, 50-51

W

weather 40-47, 64